CW00656521

PRAISE F[

"AWESOME - an absolute must read for any brand that wants to grow on social media. In a constantly changing digital space and shifting social environment, MXLTIPLY is your formula for success."

—DAN WOERHEIDE,
TRANSFORMATION COACH

"With a million things on my to-do list, I made the mistake of reading the first sentence of MXLTIPLY. I was addicted. I didn't put the book down until I devoured every last word. It's that good. And I've read a LOT of marketing books. I've been in marketing and copywriting for over four years. Every business owner knows social media is vital, but for many of us (myself included), it's far from our favorite part of our business. Bryan's system for content creation is so simple, effective, and brilliant, you'll wonder why you didn't think of it. After you read MXLTIPLY, you'll be excited to create social media content with a system that's NOT overwhelming and actually gets the results you want (to grow your biz using social). MXLTIPLY is a must-read for any serious business owner."

—DAWN APUAN, CERTIFIED
COPYWRITER AND BESTSELLING
AUTHOR OF *I RETIRED HIM*

Bryan gives us his genius wrapped in a clear how-to manual to captivate, communicate, and compete in today's online marketplace using short-form video. MXLTIPLY is welcome salve for every entrepreneur and business leader struggling for social media success

—BECKY WARNER, BUSINESS AND MARKETING CONSULTANT AT INNOVATIVE BRANDING INC. AND FOUNDER OF THRIVABLE YOU

If you are looking for a resource that will help you grab the attention of your desired audience and communicate your message with unerring aim, then Bryan's book, MXLTIPLY, is the resource you need. This book will give you a cutting-edge marketing advantage in your business.

—DR. FRED JONES, CREATOR OF BESTSELLER OVERNIGHT

As an online communicator and full-time mother, I'm always looking for ways to maximize my reach in the most time-efficient way possible. Bryan has created a framework that walks you through easy steps to do just that. His take on the social media algorithm helps you to create a non-intimidating plan to move forward with your business and your message. MXLTIPLY is a resource to keep in your back pocket and pull out any time you need a boost of social media confidence.

—JENNIFER BRYANT, AUTHOR,
DIGITAL CONSULTANT, AND
FOUNDER OF PRACTICAL FAMILY

MXLTIPLY

A SOCIAL MEDIA GUIDE FOR EVERY
ENTREPRENEUR TO CONNECT WITH A
MULTITUDE OF PEOPLE, GAIN A MASSIVE
FOLLOWING, AND MXLTIPLY YOUR SALES

BRYAN SWITALSKI

FOREWORD BY
RAY EDWARDS

Disclaimer

Although the author/publisher has made every effort to ensure that the information in this book was correct at press time and while this publication is designed to provide accurate information in regard to the subject matter covered, the author/publisher assumes no responsibility for errors, inaccuracies, omissions, or any other inconsistencies herein and hereby disclaim any liability to any party for any loss, damage, or disruption caused by errors or omissions, whether such errors or omissions result from negligence, accident, or any other cause.

This publication is meant as a source of valuable information for the reader, however, it is not meant as a substitute for direct expert assistance. If such level of assistance is required, the services of a competent professional should be sought.

In memory of Alex Michel, who helped me believe I had something valuable to offer the world.

This book comes with a free Content Planner, Social Media Prompts, and other bonuses. Scan the QR code below to access your bonuses:

CONTENTS

FOREWORD

Practically every week of the year, I receive multiple requests from authors who want to know if I would write endorsements for their books. My answer is almost universally the same: "No."

That's because I read a lot of books already and every new request for endorsement means another book added to the stack. A book I didn't ask for, didn't seek out, and didn't intend to read. Also, many of those books are terrible, and I don't think anyone wants to endorse poor quality.

MXLTIPLY is very different.

When Bryan asked me if I might consider writing a foreword for his book, it was an easy and instant "yes" on my part. The reason for this is simple: every month I write Bryan a check, he implements the method he describes in this book for my company, and that check comes back to me —multiplied—in the form of profits.

Think about what you just read.

In fact, read it again:

I write him a check, his team implements the framework for me, and that check comes back to me—multiplied—in the form of profits.

And now, in the book you hold in your hands, Bryan has given you the recipe he uses to perform this magic. Because, of course, it is not magic; it is a process, and I consider it remarkably unselfish of him to reveal his process to you, so that you can use it too.

The question is, will you do it? It is my sincere hope that you read this book, but that you don't stop there. Because merely reading the book will not help you a bit. It is the *doing* that brings the dollars.

I hope you implement the formula in this book, because it works. And whatever your message, your dream, or your brand, you deserve to have your message heard. This is the instruction book that will help you make that happen.

To Your Prosperity,
Ray Edwards
Communication Strategist

INTRODUCTION

This is not a book about becoming famous on social media. It's not about how to generate sales online. It's not about dominating the latest trends, securing the brand partnerships of your dreams, or learning how to get free advertising. But if you follow the steps in this book, you may achieve all that and more.

This is a book about communicating in a way that cuts through to the soul of your audience . . . and getting your message in front of a multitude of people who are eagerly waiting for someone—for *you*—to show up.

The truth is, your audience doesn't care about your brand. They only care about how you can help them. Once they understand how you can help, only then will they begin to resonate with you.

Your audience should be at the center of your brand, not you.

In this book, I'll lay out a framework that will change the way you think about your brand on social media and perhaps the way you do business forever.

Each year, I help brands stop wasting money on marketing, eliminate what isn't working, and grow their businesses by using proven methods. In essence, multiplying their EFFECT, not their EFFORT. This framework works for ecommerce brands, health brands, travel brands, coaches and consultants, authors, realtors, course creators, sports personalities, and even your dear old grandma (more on that later). It will work for you, regardless of your industry.

To get the most out of this, I encourage you to do three things:

1. Read the book and understand the MX Framework;
2. Create your content through the Framework; and
3. Mxltiply your EFFECT, not your effort.

Social media has changed. The old tactics don't work in this new world. If you've ever wondered why your attempts on social media have fallen flat, this is your sign.

The good news is, this doesn't have to be where your story ends.

The best is yet to come.

MOST SOCIAL MEDIA IS A WASTE OF TIME

I'll let you in on a secret . . . *I hate social media.*

You may be asking, "Bryan, why are you writing a book about social media if you hate it so much?"

The truth is, most social media is a complete waste of time. Many of the entrepreneurs I work with wonder if using social media is any good for their brand. When you start out, it can feel like screaming into a void.

On top of this, social media isn't engineered to help humans thrive. The algorithms that run our feeds have driven wedges between us. Social media is fueled by hatred and outrage. At the time of writing, a whistleblower has just revealed documented evidence about how complicit Facebook and Instagram have been in fostering this darker side.[1] They know people stay on their platforms when they are depressed, angry, and afraid.

We live in a dark world when it comes to social media. But I also believe this is an impetus for we who have any kind of light to share—to add value and be of benefit to the people we serve.

The opportunity for your message to reach a massive audience is greater than ever before—and the opportunity not just to reach anybody, but to reach people who are going to resonate deeply with your message.

Short-form video has changed the game. This shift is incredibly valuable to any brand. Its effect would be very hard or very expensive to accomplish, even with a large budget of ad dollars.

Don't get me wrong: I believe in paid advertising. But I also believe the magic that ignites the power of paid advertising is a good, real, viable presence on social media.

It's one of the most effective uses of your time and resources in terms of growing your brand.

As entrepreneurs, we should be there.

And not only should we be there to shine a light into a dark place, but there is also, I think, the best opportunity for business owners and entrepreneurs to build audiences and get customers.

Does being on social media bring new leads and conversions?

Yes. If you lead them to conversion. You can't just show up and hope they'll buy. You need a plan.

Luckily, you are reading this book. Inside, you'll find a step-by-step plan to not only grow an audience of raving fans, but also to convert them into paying customers.

This is why I write to you today. I believe good businesses deserve to have their messages heard. I believe they deserve to win. When good businesses win, people are served, jobs are created, and everyone benefits.

In the end, fame isn't what we're after . . . is it? What we're really after are the things a large platform can give us:

That feeling of confidence;

—of freedom to call our own shots;

—of predictable cash-flow;

—of serving those we care about and those in need;

—of having more options in life;

—of feeling more alive.

The stage is set.

Your audience awaits.

CHAPTER 1
AN EXPONENTIAL SHIFT OF ATTENTION

SOCIAL MEDIA ISN'T what it has been for the past decade . . . and that's a good thing.

In the old world, you could post some stuff and see a fair amount of engagement. A few likes here and there, a few friendly comments, maybe even a DM ("direct message") or two. Social media feeds were flooded with pictures of inspirational quotes, exotic destinations, exotic food from those destinations, favorite nieces or nephews, and cats being, well . . . cats.

From then on, social media became "the front page of the internet"—the source for almost all information, the latest breaking news, entertainment, live-streamed video games, and tutorials to help you fix your broken sink.

And then the algorithms changed. Suddenly, you saw less from your friends and more ads. And if you ran a professional brand or business page, your engagement started drying up. Fewer DMs and comments from your favorite customers. It didn't matter if you had a few hundred followers or a hundred thousand—the apps started to feel like ghost towns. It was like a post-apocalyptic landscape from *The Terminator*, after all the machines took over.

Two things happened:

1. the apps switched to pay-to-play models of engagement for businesses on their platforms; and
2. the feeds switched from chronological displays, where you could see everything, to displays based on weighted-interest algorithms.

If you weren't paying for ads as a business, your visibility online became pretty much non-existent. And so, brands started paying the piper.

Years later, the ads stopped working, as well. Smart-targeting options got removed. Privacy settings rolled out as the default on phones, making you invisible to advertisers. In some cases, you had to spend twice as much on ads to get the same results as the year before.

And then a miracle happened.

In the midst of a divisive election season, with people abandoning social media left and right, a new app was born.

This app was named TikTok.

On TikTok, you could post a fifteen-second video synced to your favorite music track. At first, it was just a cute app teenagers used for dancing videos and memes, but its carefree spirit and levity was such a welcome change, it kept people on the platform. As a result, it began to grow—exponentially.

But I attribute TikTok's meteoric success to one thing: *the For You page.*

Unlike other apps, in which you have to follow people to see content, TikTok's default "homepage" is full of videos from creators you've never seen. And so, the number of creators began to grow—exponentially.

It's said that, on Instagram, only 10%–12% of your following will ever see your content. This is night and day compared to TikTok, where people see your content first, then follow you.

Creators and brands from all apps started using TikTok instead. It became a new frontier.

As of the time of writing, TikTok has surpassed Instagram in monthly active users[1] (the holy grail statistic for apps), reaching **one billion**. That's a lot of people.

Even grandma is on TikTok. Don't believe me? Here are four of the top grannies of TikTok:

- @thechainzfamily
- @jrudderz
- @grandmadroniak
- @its_j_dog

The point is, it's not just for teenagers. In fact, teens only make up about 25% of TikTok users.[2] Surprising, eh?

As a result, all the other apps have taken notice and made their own TikTok clones to compete. YouTube created *Shorts*, Pinterest added *Ideas*, and Instagram created *Reels*. It's like a high-stakes game of copycat.

Head of Instagram Adam Mosseri even claimed that Instagram is "no longer a photo-sharing app," naming TikTok as one of their biggest competitors.[3] They're putting all their weight behind Reels.

Oh, and remember good ole Facebook? They're doing *Reels* too.

So what does this Game-of-Thrones-style battle for attention mean for your brand?

Simply put, as a creator on these platforms, you hold all the power. The apps want your content now more than ever and will do whatever it takes to keep you. The result? Brands are growing like never before.

But before we continue, I want to pull back the curtain on one of my marketing strategies—one that has been tested by time, no matter what the algorithms are doing.

It's this:

The Law of Preferred Placement.

CHAPTER 2
BEING VISIBLE IN A CROWDED MARKETPLACE
THE LAW OF PREFERRED PLACEMENT

THE IDEA of Preferred Placement has been around since the dawn of time. It's the article above the fold of the newspaper. It's the restaurant or gas station located on the corner of the main road. There are businesses that get more attention from customers simply because of *where they are positioned*.

So how does this translate to the digital world of social media?

On the apps it's no different. When a social media app develops a new product or feature, it pours a ton of resources into that feature's success. It also "boosts" that new feature, at the cost of the old ones.

When the head of Instagram says, "We're no longer a photo-sharing app," he is literally telling you what to do next to succeed. The Preferred Placement has shifted. Back in the old days, Preferred Placement used to be image posts; now it's short-form video.

And, as the head of Instagram, if something like TikTok is eating your lunch, you *need* this new feature to work.

Why do I say all of this? Because I've seen it proven true again and again.

At a Mastermind event in Spokane, I talked about Preferred Placement with my colleague over a wonderful crème brûlée breakfast. Intrigued, he decided to give short-form content a try. He shot his first video right there at the restaurant. It wasn't even twenty seconds long. In under an hour, he saw more engagement from that single post than he had on his account in an entire year.[1]

The truth is this: *on social media, people only find new brands because of Preferred Placement.*

Notice I said "new brands," not brands they've been following before—although Preferred Placement will put you in front of your followers more often, as well. Most brands, though, are trying to figure out how to reach new people.

To engineer success on whatever platform you choose, you have to understand two things.

PREFERRED PLACEMENT HAPPENS ON SOCIAL MEDIA FOR TWO REASONS.

The algorithms are designed to do two things above all else.

The first is to serve up more ads and acquire more users.

This means that every platform is looking to:

- get new people to serve ads to;

- make more money from advertisers;
- build new, enticing features that cause people to share the app; and
- do anything else that will increase the number of monthly active users.

On social media, *people* are the product.

The problem is, the algorithm is also trying to do something else.

It's trying to retain attention.

In order to sell more ads, it has to keep users on the app for as long as possible; in other words, it has to retain their attention.

What this means is, **if we don't position our content in such a way as to keep people engaged, the algorithm will drown it out.**

Every time someone sees your content or somebody goes to your profile, it's as though there's an invisible stopwatch that starts timing. **The less time people's eyes linger on it, the less engagement you'll see on your account.**

So that means I should create longer content to keep people watching—right?

Wrong.

NETFLIX *VS.* THE POTATO CHIP

If you asked anyone on the street where they spend the most time watching content, they would probably say Netflix.

Netflix is arguably the most-watched platform for movies and television. It is the master of the entertainment industry, skilled at keeping people on the platform for as long as possible. Social media apps are playing the same game. They too have algorithms designed to retain your attention and sell more ads to businesses.

Wait—what?!!

Sell ads? Netflix doesn't have any ads.

In July of 2016, Netflix debuted the first season of *Stranger Things.* It's perhaps one of their best original shows. This 80s-era, nostalgic series was brilliantly engineered to keep people bingeing on it—and it worked.

It was also engineered to sell Eggos. And Eggo sales *BOOMED.*

In fact, each season triggers an Eggo sales boom. According to *Business Insider*, "When *Stranger Things* Season 2 arrived on Netflix in October 2017, Eggo waffles saw the most social mentions in a single month ever. In Q4 2017, Eggo consumption saw a +14% year-on-year increase."[1]

That's a lot of Eggos.

Now, the average user's monthly time spent watching content on Netflix is 8 hours and 54 minutes (*Statista*, 13 January 2021).[2]

That's a lot of time.

But that pales in comparison to TikTok. The average user's time spent watching content on TikTok is 52 minutes PER DAY (*Oberlo*, 16 February 2021).[3]

That's 26 hours per month and nearly triple the time spent on Netflix. In the battle for our attention, TikTok is winning.

I think the reason is this: **people consume potato chips more readily than they do a whole potato.**

I haven't met a single person who hates potato chips. I've met people who try to find healthier alternatives, but no one who *hates* them. If you're reading this and you hate potato chips, send me a DM on Instagram. I would love to meet you.

Just thinking about those salty, crisp potato confections is getting me hungry.

I have, on the other hand, met people who hard-pass on a whole baked potato.

Here's what I think: *short-form content* is like potato chips. It's significantly less of an investment of time. It is much easier to consume.

I hope it's becoming clearer to you how significant this shift in human behavior is. If I asked a brand if it wanted its own Netflix show, it would leap at the opportunity in a heartbeat. Yet, something greater than Netflix has arrived, and anyone can make their own show.

Now is your time.

CHAPTER 3
EXPONENTIAL RESULTS REQUIRE EXPONENTIAL THINKING

MOST PEOPLE ARE STUCK in the trap of *analog thinking*.

Analog thinking sounds something like this: "What is this adding to or subtracting from me?"

It's simple math on a continuum with a plus or a minus at each end.

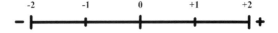

ANALOG THINKING IS black and white. If someone wins, there must be a loser. It's gain on one side and losses on the other. We do it in just about every part of life.

When it comes to marketing, the thinking goes something like this:

- How much is it going to cost?
- If I show up on one platform, I can't spend time on another.
- How much time is it going to take?
- How much money will this make?
- What if it doesn't work? What if I fail?

Now, these are all valid concerns. All of these thoughts are perfectly rational. The truth is, the Analog Continuum is only a small aspect of reality, but if it dominates our field of view, it becomes problematic.

I don't think you're stuck on the Continuum, though. Actually, I think you might be different.

You probably picked up this book because you believe there's more. Maybe your current reality isn't the one you envision for the future. If this has ever crossed your mind, you are in good company. You're on the verge of exponential thinking.

Here are some ideas worth thinking about:

- What if you could be twice as effective in a week?
- What if it took significantly less effort to do so?
- What if all it took was a single hour of your time?

I am telling you it is not only possible, but I've seen this principle proven true over and over again.

Let's do a little exponential math together. Don't worry—it will require very few math skills on your part . . . but it may stretch your thinking in a good way.

In the left column we'll add 2, and in the right column we'll multiply by 2.

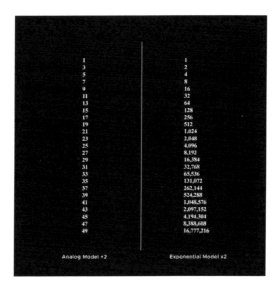

Analog Model (+2) vs. Exponential Model (x2)

Imagine your business when comparing these models. Clearly, the figures on the right are much more appealing, even if the numbers start out a little slower. (Did you notice that? Look again!)

Now imagine these figures to the power of five . . . *or even seven!* This is the foundational principle of the book you are reading.

EFFECTIVE CREATION X EXPLOSIVE CONTENT X PREFERRED PLACEMENT = EXPONENTIAL RESULTS

When my friend spent twenty seconds on his post, it got more engagement than his efforts in an entire year. What if that was *every day* for you? How would that change your business? How much more visible would your business be in the marketplace?

What is it going to cost your business if you *don't* show up?

How much more time is it going to take for you to do things the old way?

What if this actually works?

Every entrepreneur and brand must seek to **MXLTIPLY their EFFECT, not their EFFORT.**

Gary Vaynerchuck's Secret to Success

In 2019 Gary Vaynerchuck (a.k.a. Gary Vee), a well-known social media guru, published a massive 270-page deck called *How to Create 64 Pieces of Content in a Day*.[1] The title alone sounds daunting, I know, but in it he reveals the secret to his success on social media: volume.

> In a volume-centric creative world, it's about creating more context for the audience you're trying to reach and more context on the platforms that you're distributing on.
>
> GARY VAYNERCHUCK

I'm not proposing that you need to create 64 pieces of content in a day, but what most brands get wrong here is that they play favorites. They focus on building their favorite social media network and abandon the rest.

That is analog thinking at its finest.

Instead, as exponential thinkers, we can create one piece of content—*and multiply it.*

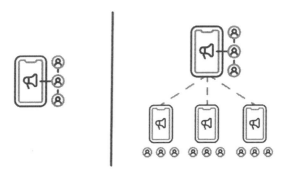

Building One Channel vs. Building Volume

In a marketplace full of noise, you need to crank up the volume.

Volume gives you an unfair advantage. Many multi-million or even multi-billion dollar brands aren't thinking exponentially. A smart brand can dwarf its competition with volume. Here are a few examples of smart brands and their followings.

Impact Theory

- 1.1M followers on Facebook
- 21K followers on Twitter
- 1.8M followers on Instagram
- 47K followers on LinkedIn
- 143.2K followers on TikTok
- 2.34M subscribers on YouTube

Jenna Kutcher

- 144K followers on Facebook
- 71.4K followers on Pinterest

- 913K followers on Instagram
- 8.831K followers on LinkedIn
- 3.54K subscribers on YouTube

Mr. Beast

- 2.1M followers on Facebook
- 11.4M followers on Twitter
- 13.7M followers on Instagram
- 22.7M followers on TikTok
- 70.8M subscribers on YouTube

You might be thinking, "Those are all great examples, but I still have to create so much content. Doesn't that take a bunch of time?"

Elon Musk's Secret to Exponential TIME

Elon Musk accomplishes more in his day than the average person. You've probably heard of him. He's the super-genius behind those sexy electric Tesla cars, who hurls Space X rockets out of the atmosphere like a madman. He was also the genius behind PayPal, before it rebranded. Surprisingly, Elon claims he's never read a single book on time management. But you don't have to be a super-genius to learn his time-saving secrets. They're actually quite simple.

Musk uses a method called Time Boxing.[2]

> If you give yourself thirty days to clean your home, it will take thirty days. But if you give yourself three hours, it will take three hours. The same applies to your goals, ambitions, and plans.

> ELON MUSK

Working with time-boxing is an important part of goal setting. You start by asking yourself, "Where do I want to be in X amount of time?" That could be one year from now, a month, or even a week.

The next step is to write down the tasks that will support your goal. So, if you want to grow on TikTok in one month, your tasks could look something like this:

1. Find the right hashtags to use.
2. Plan and write content.
3. Create a compelling caption.
4. Record content.
5. Follow up with replies and comments.

Now, instead of working on each task for as long as it takes before moving on to the next one, you will set aside a block or blocks of time to do each one. For example, you might decide to spend twenty minutes researching hashtags; then you'll move on to the next task.

Once you figure out how much time you want to allocate to each task, block it off on your calendar. By focusing on one task-block at a time, you'll gain an incredible advantage and won't waste time wandering down rabbit trails.

WHEN YOU COMBINE the principles you've learned in this chapter—Exponential Mindset, Cranking the Volume, and Time Boxing—you won't just be thinking exponentially; you will gain exponential results.

Now, onto how all this comes together . . .

CHAPTER 4

THE SIMPLE MX FRAMEWORK

IN THE FOLLOWING sections of this book, I'll dive deep into the elements of the MX Framework, showing you how each step makes your brand engaging.

For now, let's get an eagle-eye view of the Framework, so you can start to understand how it works.

THE MXLTIPLY FRAMEWORK

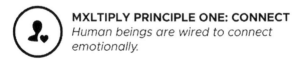

MXLTIPLY PRINCIPLE ONE: CONNECT
Human beings are wired to connect emotionally.

It is said that people don't actually buy products to solve external problems; they buy them to solve internal problems. The key here is creating emotional connection. Your message is one worth sharing, but it will fall flat without emotional connection.

In the first principle of the MX Framework, I'll show you two main ways you can connect with people on an emotional level, so people will connect with your brand.

MXLTIPLY PRINCIPLE TWO: HOOK
You only have three to five seconds to grab a person's attention.

There are billions of messages delivered on social media every day, and our brains are wired to be super-efficient at paying attention to the things we want or need. You only have three to five seconds to hook your audience before they're gone for good! It's important to provide clarity about how exactly you can help them accomplish their goals without giving them information overload—all within a short time-frame.

In the second part of the MX Framework, we'll look at the components of an effective Hook and how to use a Hook visually to compel your audience to stick around for more.

MXLTIPLY PRINCIPLE THREE: CREATE
You want your audience to watch your content all the way to the end.

It's no secret: the algorithm chooses what goes and what stays. The algorithm's main role is to keep people on the app. It promotes content that keeps users engaged. To earn brownie points with the algorithm, you want your audience to watch the whole way through.

In the third part of the MX Framework, we'll look at the three elements of viral content and how to structure content in a way that keeps people watching all the way to the end.

MXLTIPLY PRINCIPLE FOUR: SCORE
Moving the human soul through music.

A blockbuster movie wouldn't quite be the same without a good score. Music has a way of moving the human soul. Using new tools, you can communicate on a wave of emotion like never before, without having to be a musical genius like Beethoven.

In the fourth part of the MX Framework, we'll look at two ways to score your content: guiding connection and empathic connection. Each of these methods will build connections with your audience members, so they will deeply resonate with your message.

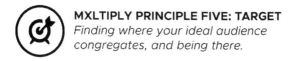

MXLTIPLY PRINCIPLE FIVE: TARGET
Finding where your ideal audience congregates, and being there.

Most content fails because it is confusing to the algorithms. The way the algorithms are built has changed. The good news is, *they're* learning from *you*. You have a direct line to the algorithm, to tell it exactly what you want.

In the fifth part of the MX Framework, I'll show you five ways to put your content directly in front of the right people —the ones who need what you have to offer.

MXLTIPLY PRINCIPLE SIX: PUBLISH
Real artists ship.

Imperfect action always beats perfect inaction. But hitting the publish button doesn't mean you will be an instant success. There are a few things most brands get wrong in this step, which can mean the difference between a few hundred and several thousand views.

In the sixth part of the MX Framework, I'll help you identify two hidden opponents trying to hinder your success and two tactics you can use to overcome them.

MXLTIPLY PRINCIPLE SEVEN: MXLTIPLY
Be fruitful and multiply.

Exponential results require exponential thinking. The brands that achieve the most success on social media are the ones who are everywhere. It's fame on a large scale. In the past, this meant having to creating a bunch of different content formats for each platform's needs. Creative hell.

In the seventh part of the MX Framework, I'll elaborate on what is perhaps the most important part of your social media strategy: being everywhere at once and building volume, without burning out on content creation.

———

WHEN YOU FEEL OVERWHELMED, MXLTIPLY YOUR EFFECT, NOT YOUR EFFORT.

Right now, you might feel like this is a lot. On your own, the challenge is not an easy one, but we can make it easier by working through the process. By following this Framework, you will be able to create content that people crave in no time.

I've created a tool to simplify the process. This easy-to use, time-saving and insightful content-creation engine will become your new best friend, because it reduces hassle by providing critical insights into what's actually working on social media for your brand—all from one simple dashboard. It's called the MX Content Engine.

You can download a printable version of the MX Content Engine for free at www.mxltiplybook.com, and it looks like this:

In the next few chapters, I'm going to walk you through the Seven Principles to help you make the MX Content Engine work for you. Once you're done, you'll no longer feel confused about how to run your social media, and you'll have content that connects deeply with existing and potential customers.

With the MX Content Engine content planner, you will be able to see your brand's content strategy on a single page, which will help you save a tremendous amount of time and grow your business.

MXLTIPLY Your Effect, Not Your Effort

While we work through the Seven Principles of the MX Framework, simply follow these three steps:

1. Read the next seven chapters;
2. Consider how you might apply each chapter to your content; and
3. Review your content ideas; then decide on a specific piece to run with.

Once you complete your content plan in your MX Content Engine, you will have the essential content you need to launch your social media strategy: all your hashtags and headlines, how you structure your content, what hooks you'll use, and how you'll transition your audience into your sales funnel. This means your content will be clear, compelling, and relevant to your audience, ultimately resulting in more sales.

It's tempting to skip parts of the Framework, since you've probably done social media before. After all, you know how it works. But many brands make the same mistakes. They make content and post it, only to see it fail. Here's why: social media is familiar to them, but they've never really grasped the mechanics behind it.

Each section of the MX Framework is designed to help you avoid the pitfalls many brands fall into around social media —pitfalls that send content straight to limbo, never to be seen by potential customers.

Every year, thousands of businesses suffer, not because their business is bad, but because they are invisible to potential customers. It's awful to build a perfect sales funnel, only to launch it and wonder where all the customers are. If you don't do the work to build an audience, you'll have to pay for expensive ads instead.

You might be thinking it's too late. After all, your competitors probably have better visibility in the marketplace. But they're not the ones reading this book. This book is designed to multiply your time, multiply the effectiveness of your content, and multiply your reach, hitting your potential customers every time. This book is your secret weapon to dwarf the competition. If you follow the principles in this book step by step, your brand will run laps around your competitors.

In the next seven chapters, I'll show you how to create compelling content that cuts through the competition, minimizes your effort, and helps grow your brand.

CHAPTER 5

CONNECT

MXLTIPLY PRINCIPLE ONE: HUMAN BEINGS ARE
WIRED TO CONNECT EMOTIONALLY.

OVER THE YEARS in Hawaii I've heard this cryptic phrase tossed around on many occasions:

"In case a bus hits me tomorrow"

What it essentially means is, "In the event I die tomorrow, this is the most important thing I want to leave you with."

Now, I'm not sure why it's a bus. I probably would have picked a shark (seems more fitting for Hawaii). I have a hard time imagining a bus prowling the streets at dusk, looking for its next victim. But, as a pedestrian, perhaps I should take this saying more seriously.

The point is this, in the event I'm not here anymore, I want to leave you with this. It's the reason I wrote this book to you. It's the reason this principle is number one.

The principle is this: ***human beings are wired to connect emotionally***.

In his book *Social Intelligence: The New Science of Human Relationships*,[1] Daniel Goleman writes:

"Even our most routine encounters act as regulators in the brain, priming our emotions, some desirable, others not. The more strongly connected we are with someone emotionally, the greater the mutual force."

But how do you connect emotionally when looking down the soulless lens of a camera?

Imagine a chair sitting in front of you. Taking a seat before you is your ideal customer—the person you want to serve. Notice the way they sit in the chair. Have they had a rough week? Are they worried about something in life right now?

You can almost look into their eyes and feel the way they are feeling. Is there something they believe that is getting in the way of the life they want to have? What do they need to hear from you?

The message you have inside you is one worth sharing. It may bring about a significant shift in the lives of many, but the truth is, without emotional connection, it will fall flat.

When you create content, there are two main ways to connect on an emotional level: empathic connection and guiding connection. You can understand these by asking yourself the following questions:

1. What kind of emotion do I want my audience to feel? (This is *guiding connection*.)
2. What are they currently feeling? (This is *empathic connection*.)

Sometimes, figuring out which emotion to pick can be a challenge. So, I like to think of emotions as a deck of cards. Each card face is an emotion.

Now, there are the more basic emotions to pick from, and there are the more complex ones. Most people know the four basic emotions: joy, sadness, anger, and fear. Yes, Pixar added a fifth in their movie *Inside Out* called Disgust,[2] but disgust is more of a "second tier" emotion, alongside anticipation, surprise, and appreciation.

You want to choose which emotion you want to lead with. This will help guide many things: which headline to use, which emojis to include, and even the tone of your delivery.

When it comes to creating content, here are some other emotions worth thinking about:

- worry;
- wonder;
- frustration;
- relief;
- confidence;
- curiosity; and
- motivation.

The next time you talk to the camera while filming your content, I want you to imagine that person sitting in the chair. Speak directly into what they are feeling and express what you want them to feel.

Being in tune with what your audience's feelings is a powerful communication technique. Being intentional about how you resonate with or lead their emotions is a skill worth developing.

If you remember anything from this chapter, I hope it's this: *leave your audience with something important, in case a bus hits you tomorrow.*

MXLTIPLY PRINCIPLE TWO: YOU ONLY HAVE
THREE TO FIVE SECONDS TO GRAB A PERSON'S
ATTENTION.

> People don't buy the best products or services; they buy
> the ones they can understand the fastest.
>
> DONALD MILLER

WE LIVE IN AN INCREDIBLY FAST-PACED,
swipe-and-scan culture. There are billions of messages
delivered on social media every day. Our brains are wired to
be super-efficient at paying attention to the things we want
and need and ignoring everything else.

The truth is, *you have three to five seconds to hook your audience—or else they're gone.*[1]

This can feel daunting.

But the good news is, you don't have to deliver *everything* in
three to five seconds . . . that would be nearly impossible.
What you need to do is get their attention.

The key here is clarity. You want to quickly tell your audience what's in it for them if they watch the rest of the video. That's it!

We call this a "hook".

Creating a good hook is kind of like baking a cake. Most people don't pass on cake unless they are *very* dedicated to their diets. I feel like passing on cake is just bad manners . . . maybe that's just me. Like any good cake, you want to include the right ingredients and leave out the spinach. Spinachy cake—yuck!

Here's a quick recipe for a good hook:

- Help identify a problem
- Reduce your audience's effort
- Eliminate the cost to accomplish something
- Reveal how to get the results they want
- Show them how to avoid the things they've been dreading.

Now, not every hook has to have all these ingredients, but a compelling hook will usually have a combination of a few.

Here are some hook templates that work incredibly well. See if you can identify some of their ingredients:

- Simple ways to do _____ for free.
- This is why your _____ isn't working.
- How I got [number] [result] in 24 hours.
- How to [result they desire most] without [thing they fear the most].

You can get more proven hooks by downloading the free companion guide at www.mxltiplybook.com

When you create your content, you want to have your hook already picked out. The first thing a person hears should be your hook statement. Not only should they hear it; they need to *SEE* it, too.

Based on a study by Verizon Media and Publicis Media, *69% of consumers are viewing video with the sound off.*[2] That's more than half!

Fortunately, most of the platforms that you can publish short-form content to have captions built in. For your hook, though, you want them to stand out. You can do this by adding a text overlay to the beginning of your video.

When adding text to your video, it's important to keep the following in mind.

1. You want your text to stand out, so go with bold colors.
2. You want a clear contrast between the text and your video. If your video is dark, choose light text, and vice versa.
3. Add an emoji reinforcing the emotion you want to lead with (surprise, frustration, amazement, shock, etc.)

Your hook can also become the thumbnail for your video. In fact, I highly recommend it. In the event someone discovers your profile and sees all the videos you have, a compelling hook will help them identify which video they should watch next.

Now go out there and serve your audience some cake!

Remember: you have three to five seconds to hook your audience—*or else they're gone.*

Download over 45+ proven hooks in the free companion guide at www.mxltiplybook.com

CHAPTER 7

CREATE

MXLTIPLY PRINCIPLE THREE: YOU WANT YOUR AUDIENCE TO WATCH YOUR CONTENT ALL THE WAY TO THE END.

THERE ARE billions of new videos uploaded to social media every day. For social media algorithms, picking the right content to show is like choosing who to play on your basketball team. You want the best players on the court.

But with billions of players, how can you ever make the cut?

I'll let you in on a secret. In the battle to get your content in front of users, there is one deciding factor almost every time.

It's called Watch-Through Rate.

A Watch-Through Rate is a measure of how long a person watches a piece of content. Did they see it, then ditch after two seconds? Did they watch it 50% of the way through or 100% of the way through?

No matter what platform your video content is on, *a high Watch-Through Rate will _always_ score you the most points.* That's because the algorithms are looking to do two things at all times:

1. serve up more ads and acquire more users; and
2. retain attention.

Social media companies will always prefer to show the content that keeps users on their platforms longer. That's what this chapter is about: *how to keep your audience watching all the way through.*

I want you to imagine the face of a clock. Maybe you've got one inside your house. I've got one, but the battery's dead. It's always stuck at 10:13 a.m. or 10:13 p.m., depending on how you look at it. When you're making your videos, I want you to think about your content like the face of the clock.

THE VIRAL CONTENT CLOCK

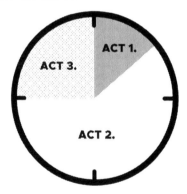

We'll divide this clock into three separate acts:

- **ACT 1:** The Hook
- **ACT 2:** The Build
- **ACT 3:** The Climax

The goal of this isn't to get the timing exact. This will work whether you've got a total of one minute or only thirty seconds. However, the tighter you can get each act, the better your content will perform.

ACT 1: THE HOOK

The first act is your hook. This is the first three to five seconds of your video. Its job is to set the stage with a promise of what the content is all about. The goal is to catch the audience's attention and move them to the next act. If you read the last chapter, you might have your hook already picked out.

Be mindful, in this act your audience is probably half-consciously scrolling through the app. This is why we cast the hook. You need them to wake up and pay full attention.

There are a couple of keys to Act 1:

- your goal is attention, not explanation;
- keep things high energy;
- use your hook headline;
- ask a question;
- include emojis in your headline; and
- start with a loud noise.

Here's a pro tip: I actually film this section last. One of the important keys to delivering a good hook is *ENERGY*. I actually have higher energy and enthusiasm toward the end of my shoots than I do at the beginning. So I capitalize on that natural energy, shoot my hook last, with enthusiasm, and then rearrange my clips in the app before publishing.

ACT 2: THE BUILD

If Act 1 is the promise, then Act 2, the longest act, delivers on that promise.

I like to think of Act 2 as three mini-acts, or "beats". The goal of each mini-act is to move a person to the next one. I might share three helpful points, present a step-by-step process, or talk about a topic from three different angles.

Act 2 can be a story; a sequence of points, tips and tricks; a list of helpful tools . . . the list goes on. Start by introducing the problem that the content of Act 2 will solve. It's a pattern of problem/solution/resolution.

In Martin Luther King Jr.'s "I have a dream" speech, Nancy Duarte identifies this pattern as a strategy for all great communicators.[1] Each beat of that speech begins with lower energy and concludes with higher energy. His speech contrasts the world that is with the world that could be. Holding the tensions between those states is a powerful communication tool.

Here are a few tips for Act 2:

- if you use the three-beats method, find a way to start each beat with a problem (the world that is);
- use elements of mystery—don't feel like you need to give away everything at once; and

- add a countdown or timer to increase the suspense and keep people watching to the end.

Remember, *your goal is to move them to the next beat.*

ACT 3: THE CLIMAX

In MLK Jr.'s speech, Act 3 is the "new norm"—the crescendo and payoff of the whole enchilada. Whatever energy level you started with in Act 1, you want to double it in Act 3. You want to paint a picture of success.

- What does life look like for your audience after their problems are solved?
- What kind of results can they expect if they use the tools or tips you shared?
- What's the next step for them to take to make this a reality?

Act 3 is a great place to ask a question or make an announcement. Maybe you have a free thing you can offer, or something to sell. The end of Act 3 is where you can finally call your audience to take action. But you don't want to be cringy about it.

Here are a few "non-cringy" calls to action you can use:

- "Check my profile for x, y, and z."
- "Tag a friend."
- "Share this with someone who . . ."
- "Tap the link in my bio to get . . ."
- "Send me a DM to . . ."
- "Get started by . . ."

If you remember anything from this chapter, I hope it's this: *a high Watch-Through Rate will <u>always</u> score you the most points.*

CHAPTER 8

SCORE

MXLTIPLY PRINCIPLE FOUR: MOVING THE HUMAN SOUL THROUGH MUSIC.

MUSIC HAS a way of moving the human soul.

One of my favorite composers is Hans Zimmer. He's known for the epic soundscapes behind some of Hollywood's most recognized films, like *Pirates of the Caribbean*, *Gladiator*, *Man of Steel*, *The Lion King*, *Wonder Woman*, and my personal favorite, *Inception*. Hans has the incredible ability to orchestrate complex, moving pieces of music that tell a story as effectively as the images on the screen.

His piece "Time" from *Inception* profoundly grips me. Sometimes I shed a tear when I'm listening to it, and to this day I don't know why.

When talking about his role in the film-making process, Zimmer said, "If you talk to any director, they'll say music is fifty percent of the movie."[1]

The same could be said of any form of video content.

For the longest time, most music that accompanied content came from the bottom of the stock-music barrel—which, let's be honest, wasn't very good. Over the years, new tools like MusicBed[2] and other services have produced higher-quality tracks for content online.

However, all of that has changed because of TikTok.

You see, at its core, TikTok is a music app.[3] That's right—a music app. Interestingly, most of the songs you hear trending on the radio are there because they started on TikTok. TikTok is not just leading the social media industry; it's leading the music industry at large.[4]

And—guess what? You as a creator have access to it all. Chances are your favorite song on the radio is there, too. Now, *should* you go picking your favorite song for your content? It's probably not the best strategy.

Instead, **SCORE *your content with the emotion you want to lead with.***

Here's what I suggest:

- pick music that evokes the feeling you want to inspire (guiding connection); or
- find music that fits what your audience might already be feeling (empathic connection).

Put on your movie-director hat. Based on the emotional connection you've decided to go for your next piece of content, pick the track that best scores the *emotion* you want to deliver.

With these new tools, you can communicate with a wave of emotion like never before.

- Do you want to deliver a somber moment of heart-

to-heart connection?
- Or perhaps an upbeat message of encouragement?
- Maybe you want to inspire action.
- Or create a calm mental space where your audience can dream about their future.

All of these and more are possible with *intentionality*.

It is great to drive emotion, but music has some other benefits, too. Using tracks puts your content in front of people who like those sounds. So if you know what your audience likes, even better!

You can choose from many tracks.

Fortunately, TikTok is really good at categorizing based on the mood you're aiming for. There are even ways of finding the highest-performing tracks for your niche. Apps like TrendTok are great for identifying early trends and excellent tracks that already resonate with your audience.[5]

The interesting thing is, not all tracks on TikTok are music.

Some are recordings people use to create video memes. Memes are powerful tools for communicating ideas in a humorous way. And humor is a great emotion to evoke. But good humor requires impeccable timing. For the sake of simplicity and effectiveness, if you're not a comedian, start with music instead.

At the end of the day, using this principle will MXLTIPLY the effectiveness of your content in more areas than one.

The principle is this: *SCORE your content with the emotion you want to lead with.*

Up next, let's talk about how you can tell the algorithms exactly who should see your content.

CHAPTER 9

TARGET

MXLTIPLY PRINCIPLE FIVE: FINDING WHERE
YOUR IDEAL AUDIENCE CONGREGATES, AND
BEING THERE.

NOW THAT YOU'VE got a valuable piece of content,
how do you get it in front of your ideal audience? Fortunately, this part is easy, and I'll tell you why . . .

*YOU get to tell the algorithms exactly what your content is
about, AND who should see it.*

The way the algorithms are built has changed. They used to
be robots. Now they run on AI (artificial intelligence).

Think of the algorithms like you would a toddler. They're
smart, but they are in the process of learning. The good
news is you get to be the teacher. And it's probably easier
than you think.

The way you teach the algorithms is with hashtags.

The truth is, the old way of doing hashtags is over. In the past, you would have to pick out 30 hashtags for every social media post. That's a lot of hashtags. But if you use that same tactic today, you will confuse the algorithms.[1] In fact, on TikTok, you can't even fit in that many hashtags.

The sweet spot is about three-to-five highly focused hashtags.[2]

Three to five hashtags isn't a lot, so here are some questions to help you find the best ones:

- What is this piece of content about, specifically?
- How do your audience members identify themselves? (Are they artists, freelancers, entrepreneurs, etc.?)

Fortunately, the tools available to you will show you which hashtags to go for on the different platforms. On TikTok, when you type in a hashtag, it will show you exactly how many *views* it gets, alongside some suggested hashtags. On

Instagram, it's basically the same, except that it shows you how many *posts* share that hashtag.

So, how many views are we going for, here? Well, that entirely depends on your stage of growth.

9,000 followers or less: Choose relevant hashtags from 50k–500k views.

10,000 followers or more: Choose relevant hashtags from 50k–5 million views.

THE DOS AND DON'TS OF HASHTAGS

People go crazy with hashtags. You really don't have to get super-creative here. However, using the wrong hashtags can get your content sucked into a blackhole, never to be seen again. Here are a few ground rules to provide you with some healthy boundaries, so you don't end up in Hashtag Limbo.

The Dos ✅:

- **Do** use hashtags that are related to your content's topic.
- **Do** check to see what hashtags your ideal audience uses and follows.
- **Do** use both well-known and niche hashtags to get more people to see your posts.
- **Do** create and use your own branded hashtags, so your fans can easily search for your content.
- **Do** keep the number of hashtags between three and five.

The Don'ts ❌:

- **Don't** use hashtags that are unrelated to your content (e.g. #explorepage, #fyp, #foryoupage).
- **Don't** use a hashtag that is too generic. It will make it hard for people to find your content.
- **Don't** use too many hashtags. If you add 10 or 20, it won't help you get more people seeing your post.
- **Don't** dump your hashtags in the comments. Keep them in the description, instead.

HOW TO DISCOVER HIGHLY FOCUSED HASHTAGS

There are basically five categories of hashtag. Like in any good recipe, you want a combination of these ingredients. You just need to know what kind of ingredients you want to include in the recipe. Too much of any one of them and the cake won't bake. The five hashtag categories are:

1. Broad
2. Identity
3. Content Niche
4. Branded
5. Location

1. The Broad Hashtag

The broad hashtag is the big-bucket category your content fits in. It's not the same thing as a generic hashtag. It's not bad to have a broad hashtag. A broad hashtag is like the flour in your cake. You only need one of these, otherwise you'll end up with a flavorless cake.

Here are some examples of broad hashtags in different industries:

> #localbusiness
> #copywriting
> #desserts
> #parenting
> #travel

2. The Identity Hashtag

Identity hashtags are some of my favorites. These can be a bit harder to find, but they are very effective. This kind of hashtag tells the algorithm *exactly who should see* this piece of content. A great way to find an identity hashtag is by jumping in your customer's shoes and completing this sentence: "I am a _____."

Here are some examples:

> #freelancer
> #copywriter
> #bakingqueen
> #parentslife
> #travelcouple

3. The Content Niche Hashtag

The content-niche hashtag is where you have the most leverage. These hashtags are super-specific to the piece of content you are sharing. You want to tell the algorithm *exactly what's inside* this piece of content.

Here are some examples:

> #freelancerbookkeepingtips
> #passiveincomefromhome
> #chocolatecupcakes

#internetsafetyforkids
#hikingadventures

4. The Branded Hashtag

The branded hashtag is something you might want to use after you have your first 1,000 followers. This involves creating a hashtag that no one else uses yet—one unique to your brand. What you are doing is transferring the views of your content to a new hashtag that you control.

You want to be getting thousands of views of your content before employing this tactic. This syphons the audience behind the hashtags you're already using into a single, branded hashtag. You are teaching the algorithm "a new word," and you're telling it exactly what it means—ultimately creating your own niche.

One of my new branded hashtags is #switalskimethod (my last name). No one else has it. It's associated with hashtags like #marketing, #entreprenuership, and #contenthacks. I've already had a few thousand views from that hashtag alone.[3]

5. The Location Hashtag

If you're a local business or want to crack into a local marketplace, this is perhaps one of the best-kept secrets: the location hashtag. By using a location hashtag, you're telling the algorithm *where your audience is*. This means that devices in the local area you target (who share an interest in your other hashtags) will start seeing your content immediately. City names or local landmarks are great selections. *Bonus points if your content is shot and uploaded in the area.*

REMEMBER: *the key to targeting is to teach the algorithm what your content is about.* To do this, we have to be specific about *what* we are showing to *whom*. If you train the algorithm well, it may become your best friend.

In the next chapter, I'll teach you how to publish your content effectively, so you can avoid the major mistakes most brands make.

CHAPTER 10

PUBLISH
MXLTIPLY PRINCIPLE SIX: REAL ARTISTS SHIP.

HERE'S where you tie it all together. This is the moment where all your pieces of work get to play together like a symphony orchestra at an opera hall. By now you should have:

- chosen your guiding/empathic emotion;
- written your compelling hook;
- created your content using the Three-Act Viral Content Clock;
- picked your score; and
- selected three to five highly focused hashtags.

This is the foundation for effective content. All of this can be done within a single hour of your time.

Congratulations for making it this far! Now that you know the pattern, we can multiply your effectiveness by plotting out a week of content in advance. I know this can sound a little overwhelming. But, trust me, it actually multiplies your time and minimizes your effort.

Here's what plotting a week's worth of content looks like.

1. Write down five ideas you want to communicate this week (this can take five minutes or less; you don't need to overthink it)
2. Next to each idea, write the guiding/connecting emotion you want to convey (five minutes)
3. Pick your hook for each idea (five minutes)
4. You've already gotten Act 1 down, so write your Act 2. A few short sentences or supporting bullet points will work perfectly (give yourself five minutes for each)
5. Write a one-sentence Act 3 for each video. What's the next action step? Or what does success look like if they follow your advice? (Five to ten minutes in total)

That's it! See, that wasn't so hard.

You might be wondering, "Why only five pieces of content for a week?" I'll share more on that later in this chapter. For now, there are only a few more steps to take to zip this up.

After filming your first video, you'll want to add the score. If you've got a voiceover or are talking to the camera in the video, you'll want to set your voice-recording volume as high as possible (100–200%). Depending on the track, you'll want to set your musical score lower, so it doesn't make your voice hard to hear (usually set at 15–20%).

Next up are your hashtags. You'll want to add the hashtags you've already researched to your content description. Remember to use three-to-five highly focused hashtags.

Next you'll create your thumbnail. You'll want to paste your hook here. Don't worry if the words take up most of the thumbnail's screen. The point here is to communicate what your video is about. Bonus points if you add an emoji to match your content's niche or the emotion you want to convey.

FINAL STEP: PUBLISH OR SAVE TO DRAFTS.

You can choose to publish today or save to drafts. If you're batch-creating, the drafts feature is your best friend. You can save your current video as a draft and jump right into creating a new piece of content. Remember Time Boxing? This comes in really handy here, and puts you in a state of flow.

———

THERE YOU ARE. From start to finish, you've designed a week's worth of short-form video content. If you're feeling extra ambitious, you could even do a whole month's. The key to this is Time Boxing. Just add more of the same tasks to each block of time. You'll be amazed how much you get done.

Now, why only five pieces of content a week? Don't you need to be posting every single day?

Here's my simple answer: no. Let me tell you why.

WHY I DON'T PUBLISH ON WEEKENDS

Let me pull back the curtain on something that doesn't get talked about often, but can severely impact your content.

Remember the algorithms are looking to do two things at all times:

1. serve up more ads and acquire more users; and
2. retain attention.

One of the main ways they do this is by engineering their platform so people get addicted. Tristan Harris, a computer scientist and one of the featured voices in the Netflix documentary *The Social Dilemma* shares:

> "More and more of our work was about manipulating people into getting their attention and less about what's really good for people.
>
> A person is worth more if they're addictively checking their phone like a slot machine. Sometimes you pull that slot machine, sometimes you get something nice—you get those five new likes or rewards. Other times you pull that refresh and you don't get anything. It's that randomness that makes it so addictive."[1]

Social media platforms simply distract their users by getting them consumed with their own consumption.

Well, this goes for you as a creator, as well. We all play the game. Just like a slot machine in Vegas, your content will ride a roller-coaster of great wins and losses—by design.

With each peak comes a valley. The thrilling rush of views and engagement one day, only to return to an empty wasteland the very next day. It's designed to keep you hooked.

Understanding this aspect of the game is key to playing against your opponent (the algorithm).

As a creator, I have two tactics to help you:

1. implementing a "Digital Sabbath"; and
2. being "contently disconnected."

IMPLEMENTING A DIGITAL SABBATH

I choose a day or two to not post on or engage with social media. Sounds crazy, right? Wouldn't it make more sense to post every single day?

It is said, after six days of creating the world, God decided to rest on the seventh day. I think there is some wisdom there for all of us. Rest is a good thing. Taking time for self-care is a good thing. It's fuel for the creative process.

This ancient wisdom also applies to the digital realm.

The algorithms want you attached. They will penalize good content just to keep you hooked. When your own content is being played against you, you need to play a different game. The key is to get off the roller coaster.

When you take a break, the algorithms shift gears and decide to play "welcoming party" for your brand. I've seen content surge using this tactic alone.

This next tactic will help you thrive no matter what your "opponent" throws your way.

BEING CONTENTLY DISCONNECTED

There is an invisible opponent in cahoots with the algorithms. It thrives on insatiable discontentment, consumption, and fear . . . all things the algorithms are built to serve. It sees and hears everything you do.

It's the Big Boss at the end of the game.

It's YOU—well, kind of.

You might be wondering, "What in the Scooby Doo is going on here?"

Everyone has what is called a "digital shadow," sometimes referred to as a "doppelgänger."[2] It's a digital model of you, comprised of every bit of data the internet knows about you. It's like your own personal clone in the digital realm.

The problem with this is your digital shadow inherits your best and your worst qualities. Then, your worst qualities get played against you. That's how each algorithm knows how to concoct its own special recipe to keep you addicted.

To combat this opponent as a creator, we must adopt higher qualities instead of falling into its codependent trap.

I call one of these higher qualities **"being contently disconnected."**

You see, if the algorithm wants you emotionally connected to the outcome of your content, the secret is to become detached.

Instead of playing the game for "views," we can play the game for the sake of the people we want to serve. Yes, views are important, but they're not the true goal. If the true goal were simply views, there are a lot of ways of getting there (often involving bikinis). Our true goal and true source of joy must be bigger than empty views.

Here's an example:

- **Being discontentedly connected:** *Wow, I only got 150 views on my video . . . it must suck.*
- **Being contently disconnected:** *Wow, I got 150 views on my video! That means 150 people got to hear my message . . . that's more people than I talk to in a single day!*

Can you see the difference? It's a subtle shift into gratitude, reinforcing the joy we have—our fuel to see things through.

In the next chapter, I'll share with you the critical difference between content that gets zero views and multiplying the content you've already created to hit millions of people. Hold on to your seat—this is going to rock your world!

MXLTIPLY PRINCIPLE SEVEN: BE FRUITFUL AND MULTIPLY.

AN AUTHOR FRIEND of mine looked at me, shocked. She'd just posted her TikTok video to Reels. It was announcing the brand-new book she was releasing to the world. On Reels, though, it got ZERO views. What went wrong? Did the algorithms hate her book that much?

The problem wasn't with her message. It wasn't an issue with the connection she was creating with her audience. *Why zero views?*

I took a quick look at the video and instantly knew what went wrong. The truth is, the problem was with her content, but not in a way you would expect.

It had a TikTok logo watermark.

This is one of the biggest mistakes brands make when they repurpose content. The algorithms are built to sniff out a competitor's watermark like bloodhounds.[1]

It's the same across all the platforms.

It makes sense. Why would you want your competitor's logo all over the content you're serving up to your users? That's free advertising for the opposition!

After a minute spent reposting a watermark-free version, her new video got more than 3,000 views in under two hours.

So, if there's one critical thing you want to remember before posting . . .

Don't share watermarked content.

So, how do you download a watermark-free version of your latest video? There are a bunch of apps and websites to help you download your content watermark-free. When it comes to TikTok, I like using the snaptik.app website.[2] You just paste your content's link, hit the download button, and *voila*! You've got yourself a watermark-free version of your video.

You've got your watermark-free video. What do you do next? We're going to assume you started with TikTok to create your video (but you can create your videos however you'd like). From there, you're going to distribute to the other main platforms that support short-form content:

- YouTube Shorts
- Instagram Reels
- Pinterest Ideas
- Facebook Reels
- LinkedIn Video

YOUTUBE SHORTS

YouTube Shorts is incredibly easy to set up.[3] You can use the app or the website. You can even schedule your content in advance. With Shorts you can have a full sixty seconds of content. You'll need three things to publish to Shorts:

1. your watermark-free video (sixty seconds or less);
2. a compelling headline for your video title; and
3. the hashtag #shorts added to the end of your video title.

INSTAGRAM REELS

Instagram Reels is a lot like TikTok.[2] You'll need the Instagram app to post a Reel. It also gives you the option to publish the Reel to your feed (I recommend doing so). For Instagram Reels you'll need:

1. your watermark-free video (sixty seconds or less);
2. a compelling headline for your description; and
3. three-to-five niche hashtags.

Note: If you have your Instagram connected to your Facebook, sometimes the option to publish to both simultaneously is available.[5]

FACEBOOK REELS

Facebook Reels is very new and still being ironed out.[6] It works much like Instagram Reels. They just rolled out the ability to upload 30 seconds of content, so if your audience is on Facebook, Facebook Reels is a great option. You'll need the following for Facebook Reels:

1. your watermark-free video (thirty seconds or less); and
2. a compelling headline for your description.

PINTEREST IDEAS

Pinterest really is my first love. It's more like a search engine than a social network.[7] In the past, Pinterest was a bit more of a long game, like most search engines are. With Pinterest Ideas you can draw instant attention to your content. In fact, if you have a multiple-part series of videos, you can combine them together in the same "Idea."[8] You'll need the following for Pinterest Ideas:

1. your watermark-free video(s) (sixty seconds or less);
2. a compelling headline for your title;
3. a relevant Pinterest board to share it to; and
4. topic tags relevant to your video (think of this as like hashtags, but you can only select what they've got available).

Note: With Pinterest Ideas, your file will need to be under a minute, otherwise it won't upload.[9]

LINKEDIN VIDEO

LinkedIn Video is very easy. From the app, just upload your video.[10] You'll need the following:

1. your watermark-free video (ten minutes or less);

2. a compelling headline for your description; and

3. three-to-five niche hashtags.

———

REPOSTING to any one of these platforms takes less than five minutes. Once you've gotten into the flow, it's usually about one minute each. If you're using all five of these channels, then, it's all done in ten to twenty minutes. It's a simple task.

If you want to multiply your time even further, I recommend hiring a virtual assistant (a "VA") who can post for you. Hiring a VA will multiply your time, so you can focus on your "zone of genius."

Each of the short-form video platforms listed will outperform all other forms of social media content because of the Law of Preferred Placement.

EFFECTIVE CREATION X EXPLOSIVE CONTENT X PREFERRED PLACEMENT = EXPONENTIAL RESULTS

That's the MXLTIPLY Framework. If you follow each step of the framework, you will:

> MXLTIPLY your time
> MXLTIPLY your effect
> MXLTIPLY your results

On to one of the most common questions I get asked: *can you actually get sales through social media?*

CHAPTER 12
THE SECRETS TO SOCIAL SELLING

I GET ASKED this question all the time: *Do people buy on social media?* I am personally shocked at the lack of books available on this topic.

The answer is YES!

According to Tubular Insights, **64% of consumers make a purchase** after watching branded social videos.[1] Wow! "Makes a *purchase*." Good for those folks who use video —right?

That's why in this chapter we're going to look at how to MXLTIPLY your sales using social media.

Selling on social media takes intentionality.

When selling on social media, most brands will create their product/service, build a beautiful sales funnel . . . and wait until it's finished to announce it to the world in a single post. This is what most brands get wrong about social selling.

This would be like Hollywood sharing the trailer to its next movie *only after* theaters are able to sell tickets. That movie probably wouldn't sell very well, would it?

Nevertheless, time and again businesses make this mistake.

SECRET #1: THE HOLLYWOOD METHOD FOR BLOCKBUSTER SALES

When Hollywood breaks out its next blockbuster, it's showing trailers for *years* before it comes out (long before the movie is even finished filming).

I'm actually looking forward to the next Spider-Man film. Why? *I saw a trailer for it!*

This is how I want you to think about social selling. **If your product is "the movie," your social media content is "the trailer."** You want to talk about your product/service well in advance. It creates desire for what you're going to offer.

You might be scratching your head right now: "If my product isn't ready, how do I talk about it?"

I think Apple is a great example. They're talking about what they're cooking up sometimes two years before their next product is finished. What Apple's marketing did well in the Steve Jobs era was to focus on ideas, rather than product.[2]

They would talk about who you are and how their product would enhance what you could become. They focused on the things that mattered to their customers, like having more of their favorite music in their pocket.[3]

So, how can you, practically, create desire for a product/service that doesn't exist yet?

- Talk about *who* your audience is. How do they see themselves? What do they aspire to become?
- Talk about *why* you care about them. It's said that people don't care about what you have to say until they understand how much you care about them.
- Talk about their *problem*. Create content around what's keeping them up at night (which your product/service will be there to solve).
- Talk about *what* a day in their life looks like. How could it be different if they had your awesome solution?

What if I have a product already? Is it too late?

It's never too late to talk about your product/service on social media. Like the examples, however, you want to talk more about your audience and their lives than you do your offer. Your solution itself isn't the point. Solving their problem and helping them succeed is.

Once you've created your trailer-style content, what's the next step?

SECRET #2: APPLE'S SUPER-SECRET BILLION-DOLLAR SALES FUNNEL

Two of my favorite stores are Costco and Apple. Both offer high-ticket products ($500+). They both have great ratings and, overall, a pretty great customer experience. In both stores you can sample their products. (Arguably, Costco's samples are more tasty.) Both hold products you and I use every single day.

Here's what's crazy. Apple brings in *more than ten times* the revenue that Costco does. At the end of the day, it's not actually the size of the store or how many products they have that brings in the sales. What Apple does better than anyone else is their invisible sales funnel.

They make it stupidly easy to purchase from them.

When you go to Costco, you have to wander around to find what you want. Oftentimes things are moved (intentionally) to a completely different aisle. The idea there is to get you to walk the store and bump into products you normally wouldn't, so you buy more stuff.

Can you guess what Costco's best-selling product is? It's actually their roasted chicken.[4] They know this, which is why they sell it so cheaply. They actually don't make profit on their best-selling product.

Apple's store is much smaller. The products often change. Sometimes they move things around the store. Interestingly, they rarely ever discount their products. But here's what you don't see there: wandering.

Apple has made it so you don't have to wander aisles to find what you're looking for. They will greet you at the door, find out what you want, and help you get it, without any hassle. *Only after* you've found what you want will they "upsell" (usually an accessory that goes with the product). It's frictionless spending.

You don't want to be the department store; you want to be the Apple Store.

This is the big mistake most brands make on social media. The link in their bio is usually to the homepage of their website, and you have to wander around to find what you're looking for. They force their followers through too many clicks.

This is like hiding the cash register in a store. Ain't nobody got time for that. As the saying goes: *a confused mind will always say, "No."*[5]

So how do you get people to buy from you?

What you need is a simple sales funnel. You want to eliminate the clicks required for people to get what they want. Make it easy to buy from you. Less clicks = more purchases.[6]

If you're selling a product, link directly to that product. On some of these platforms like TikTok, Instagram, and Pinterest, each piece of content can actually be linked to directly. This means that, while a potential customer is listening to you talking about it, they can purchase it right there on the spot. How awesome is that?

But what if people aren't ready to buy yet?

SECRET #3: THE ALCHEMIST'S GOLDEN FORMULA

What I'm about to share with you is an ancient secret all great marketers know: the alchemy of turning your audience members into customers.

Everyone has an audience. It might be a small audience, but it's an audience, nonetheless. You don't actually need a gigantic audience to make sales.

Here's the problem: if one of these social media networks decides to kick you off their platform, it doesn't matter how many followers you *had*—poof! They are gone. This can happen from time to time, even if you haven't done anything wrong.

On September 4th, 2021, all the Facebook platforms (Facebook, Instagram, Messenger, and WhatsApp) went dark for about six hours.[7] Nobody knew what was going on. Ad campaigns dried up completely. There was panic in the streets! (Well, not in the actual streets.) What brands figured out very quickly is that you can't put all your eggs in one basket.

What you really need is an audience that you own.

The social media networks don't give you your followers' contact information, so you need to transfer your audience from social media to a list of contacts that you own. This could be an email list, a text-message list, or a members area where you can communicate directly with your customers and potential customers.

So how do you get this information from your audience? You need to offer something valuable in exchange for their information. We call this a "lead generator."

A lead generator delivers value and captures lots of new and potential customers.

What is a lead? A lead is a person in your audience who decides to engage with your brand and give you their information before they make a purchase.

Think of this like a dating relationship, leading to marriage. This gives your potential customer the time they need to get to know you better and understand how your product/service can help them, before they commit. We call this process "lead nurturing."

"Leads who are effectively nurtured produce a **20% increase in sales**" (source: demandgen).[8] Anybody want a 20% increase in sales this year? Hi! Me!

But first we have to offer them something valuable (often for free). This is the "lead generator."

A lead generator (a.k.a. "lead magnet" or "lead gen") can be anything of value you give away for *free*, such as:

- a white paper or PDF download;
- educational videos;
- toolkits or resource lists;
- podcasts or webinars;
- quizzes, surveys, or worksheets;
- discounted or free samples of your product;
- the ability to "test drive" your product or service;
- a few pages from your new book; or
- limited-time free trials.

All of these are relevant and powerful tools in today's fast-paced, competitive market. But why bother? What's the point?

Including a lead generator in your social selling strategy increases your authority in the minds of potential customers —it displays your competence as a guide they can trust to help them solve their problems.

Then, when they are ready to buy, guess who they will look to first?

A lead-generator page is super-simple to use. I'd recommend a simple form requesting their first name and their email. To make this even easier, I've built one of these page templates for you.

You can download this simple social-sales-funnel template for free at www.mxltiplybook.com

I actually recommend using your lead generator as your main link in your bio. It is a powerful tool to help you build trust and authority and position your business as a value-first brand. Think of your lead generator as that helpful greeter at the door of the Apple Store.

THE SOCIAL SALES FUNNEL

Now that you've added them to a list, you need to nurture this relationship. Good relationships are built on good communication. The best approach is to create a series of messages (via either text or email) to help build the relationship and seal the deal.

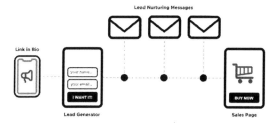

I recommend a simple follow-up message-sequence to help nurture the relationship:

- **Message 1 (send instantly):** deliver the free good(s) they requested.
- **Message 2 (send after 24 hours):** talk about the problem they are facing that your paid offer will solve. Link to your sales page.
- **Message 3 (send on day two):** overcome some of their common objections with ways your offer will change their life. Link to your sales page.
- **Message 4 (send on day three):** share a story from one of your clients about how your product/service changed their life. Link to your sales page.
- **Message 5 (send on day four):** deliver your sales letter. Hit the problem. Overcome objections. Share a testimony. Close with a strong call to action to buy today. Link to your sales page.

If you want to learn how to craft compelling messages that cause people to buy, I highly recommend the book *How to Write Copy That Sells*[9] by my friend Ray Edwards.

You need a sales funnel. When you intentionally guide people through an intentional sales process, you will start selling on social media.

AFTERWORD

For as long as I can remember I've wanted to be an author, but never in my wildest dreams did I think I would become a BEST-SELLING AUTHOR.

Well . . . it turns out that is not *altogether* true.

I looked back through my Life Plan again this morning, and one of my wildly ambitious five-year goals was to be a best-selling author. My jaw hit the floor when I read that. I'd completely forgotten about it.

It turns out your wildest dreams do come true.

But they don't happen by accident. This book got into your hands because of social media. My message was able to hit the right people at the right time because I used the techniques I've laid out for you in the book you are now holding.

I share this not because I want you to think I'm awesome. I share this because I want you to see what is possible for *you*.

The things that used to be dreams can become reality.

Over the next few years I'll be working closely with entrepreneurs who dare to live out their wildest dreams by multiplying their EFFECT on the world instead of their effort. Maybe that's you. In any case, I hope this book helps you believe in what is possible, and provides practical tools to help you achieve it.

Here's to dreaming bigger.

May your wildest dreams come true, too.

ACKNOWLEDGMENTS

I'm grateful for the people who came alongside me to make this book possible. Success doesn't happen in a vacuum, and neither do good books.

To Ray Edwards—years ago you said we should collaborate on something, and here we are. I am truly honored. You model for me what it looks like to build a business intentionally and with the highest integrity. It's been a joy to work with you and your team. I live a more inspired and prosperous life because of your influence.

To my book coach, Dr. Fred Jones—for believing in my worth and not settling for less. I appreciate your passion and genuine conviction to see the best in people realized . . . and to help people with a message become Best Sellers Overnight. You, sir, are a genius.

To my editor, Danica Issell—for helping me sound smart and being part of making this book a reality.

To Becky Warner, for your extensive notes, helping to polish this book into what it is today.

To Dean Kaneshiro—for all the conversations, years of partnership, and true testing of our wildest marketing ideas. You entered my life at a critical point, and I treasure our friendship dearly.

To Creighton Arita—who invested in me and set a paradigm of entrepreneurship unto greater impact and greater good. You create a sandbox for people to develop into who they are called to be, long before many can see it for themselves.

To my friend Hunter Hughes, The All Around Athlete—who embodies many of the paradigms in this book—and was doing so long before it was written—and models for so many what it looks like to be a creator rather than a consumer. Thank you for bearing with me through our many marketing conversations and the constant slew of TikTok memes. You are a true friend.

Finally, to you, the reader, for picking up this book. You are the reason I wrote it.

APPENDIX 1
SOCIAL MEDIA AUDIT

We've included space to do your own Social Media Audit in this section of the book. With this checklist you can identify what's working well and discover critical actions you can take to massively improve your marketing.

You can download these pages for free and print off as many copies of them as you like. Just visit www.mxltiplybook.com or use the QR code in the beginning of this book.

Please answer the following questions on behalf of your brand:

————

WHAT PLATFORMS IS YOUR BRAND ON?

[ ] Instagram

[ ] TikTok

[ ] Pinterest

[ ] Youtube

[ ] LinkedIn

[ ] Facebook

YOUR SOCIAL BIO

[ ] Is your bio clear about what problem you help people solve?

[ ] Is your bio clear about what success looks like for your audience?

[ ] Is there a clear call to action in the bio?

[ ] Do you have a link in your bio?

[ ] Is there something you offer for free when they click the link?

[ ] When someone clicks your link, are you collecting their email?

YOUR PROFILE PHOTO

[ ] Are you using a clear photo of you?

[ ] Are you using your primary brand color in your profile photo?

YOUR CONTENT THUMBNAILS

[ ] Are you using headline in your video thumbnails?

[ ] Is the headline legible? (not covered by video view numbers or cropped off screen)

[ ] Does the thumbnail show your face?

[ ] Is the headline clear? (Free of acronyms or insider language)

[ ] Is your headline compelling? (Does it create curiosity)

[ ] Does your thumbnail include an emoji?

YOUR CONTENT

[ ] Are you using closed captions? (For when people have audio on mute)

[ ] Are you using a text headline at the beginning of your video?

[ ] Is your text clear of the UI? (UI includes the icons on the right and the description below)

[ ] Is your text legible?

[ ] Are you using a hook in the first 3-5 seconds of the video?

[ ] Are you using a clear Call to Action at the end of your video?

———

Congratulations for completing this Social Media Audit! I'd love to see your before and after results! Want to learn more helpful tips from me? Follow me on:

Instagram: @bswisshd

TikTok: @bswisshd

If you want help MXLTIPLY your effect on social media, I can help coach you or your team. You can simply connect with me through a DM or at leverageclarity.com

APPENDIX 2
CONTENT TOPIC
BRAINSTORMING

Whenever you use social media to promote a product then use this worksheet to create content that provides value to the viewer and sells the product without being salesy. Ask questions and provide information that your viewer will relate to and aim to initiate a discussion which creates even more post engagement.

———

List specific problems your product or service solves:

....

....

....

....

What is the end goal your customers are looking for? (i.e. sleep better, weight loss etc).

_____

What are some benefits your audience want to see? (i.e. more followers, more free time etc).

_____

What pain points does the problem cause? (i.e. no money, always working, weight gain etc).

_____

What emotions does this problem makes them feel?

_____

What are some results they will see when they solve this problem?

_____

What are some consequences they will experience if they do not take action now?

What positive life changes they will have once they solve this problem?

List the simple steps they need to take in order to solve this problem:

What are things to avoid and obstacles they may experience while trying to solve this problem?

NOTES

INTRODUCTION

1. Bobby Allyn, "Here are 4 key points from the Facebook whistleblower's testimony on Capitol Hill," NPR, Oct 5, 2021, https://www.npr.org/2021/10/05/1043377310/facebook-whistleblower-frances-haugen-congress

CHAPTER 1: AN EXPONENTIAL SHIFT OF ATTENTION

1. Marisa Dellatto, "TikTok Hits 1 Billion Monthly Active Users," Forbes, Sep 27, 2021, https://www.forbes.com/sites/marisadellatto/2021/09/27/tiktok-hits-1-billion-monthly-active-users/
2. Statista Research Department, "Distribution of TikTok users in the United States," Statista, Jan 27, 2021, https://www.statista.com/statistics/1095186/tiktok-us-users-age/
3. Mitchell Clark, "Head of Instagram says Instagram

is no longer a photo sharing app," The Verge, Jun 30, 2021, https://www.theverge.com/2021/6/30/22557942/instagram-no-longer-photo-app-video-entertainment-focus

CHAPTER 2: BEING VISIBLE IN A CROWDED MARKETPLACE

1. Carrie Wittmer, "Netflix's 'Stranger Things' boosted Eggo waffle sales because one of the main characters is obsessed with them," Insider, Feb 21, 2018, https://www.businessinsider.com/netflixs-stranger-things-boosted-eggo-waffle-sales-2018-2

2. Julia Stoll, "The average user's monthly time spent watching content on Netflix is 8 hours and 54 minutes," Statista, Jan 18, 2022, https://lb-aps-frontend.statista.com/statistics/325055/time-spent-viewer-watching-netflix-usa/

3. Maryam Mohsin, "The average user's time spent watching content on TikTok is 52 minutes per day," Oberlo, Feb 16, 2021, https://www.oberlo.com/blog/tiktok-statistics

CHAPTER 3: EXPONENTIAL RESULTS REQUIRE EXPONENTIAL THINKING

1. Garyvee, "How to Make 64 Pieces of Content in a Day," Gary Vaynerchuk, Nov 14, 2019, https://www.garyvaynerchuk.com/how-to-create-64-pieces-of-content-in-a-day/

2. Christian Soschner, "This One Time Management Method Makes Elon Musk the Most Successful Entrepreneur," Data Driven Investor, Sep 3, 2020,

https://medium.datadriveninvestor.com/this-one-time-management-method-makes-elon-musk-the-most-successful-entrepreneur-1af5a0ad507a

CHAPTER 5: CONNECT

1. Daniel Goleman, "Social Intelligence: The New Science of Human Relationships," Social Intelligence: The New Science of Human Relationships
2. Rachael Bedford Ph.D., "The Science of Emotion From the Inside Out," Psychology Today, Dec 15, 2017, https://www.psychologytoday.com/us/blog/if-babies-could-talk/201712/the-science-emotion-the-inside-out

CHAPTER 6: HOOK

1. Joshua Conran, "How to Grab Your Target's Attention in 8 Seconds (or Less)," Inc., Oct 13, 2014, https://www.inc.com/joshua-conran/how-to-grab-your-target-s-attention-in-8-seconds-or-less.html
2. TJ McCue, "Verizon Media Says 69 Percent Of Consumers Watching Video With Sound Off," Forbes, Jul 31, 2019, https://www.forbes.com/sites/tjmccue/2019/07/31/verizon-media-says-69-percent-of-consumers-watching-video-with-sound-off/

CHAPTER 7: CREATE

1. Nancy Duarte, "The secret structure of great talks,"

TEDxEast, Nov 2011, https://www.ted.com/
talks/nancy_duarte_the_secret_structure_of_great_t
alks

CHAPTER 8: SCORE

1. Joel Beckerman, "You Don't Have To Understand
   Music To Feel Its Power," Time, Dec 20, 2014,
   https://time.com/3531708/sonic-boom-music-theme/
2. MusicBed, https://www.musicbed.com/
3. TikTok, "TikTok Launches New Music Hub,"
   TikTok Newsroom, Mar 10, 2021, https://newsroom.
   tiktok.com/en-gb/tiktok-launches-new-music-hub
4. Dan Whateley, "How TikTok is changing the music
   industry," Business Insider, Updated Jan 3, 2022,
   https://www.businessinsider.com/how-tiktok-is-
   changing-the-music-industry-marketing-
   discovery-2021-7
5. Marlen Hüllbrock, "Tools. TrendTok: #1 app for
   TikTok Trends & Sounds," Musically, Apr 1, 2021,
   https://musically.com/2021/04/01/tools-trendtok-1-
   app-for-tiktok-trends-sounds/

CHAPTER 9: TARGET

1. Christina Newberry, "2021 Instagram Hashtag
   Guide: How to Get More Reach," Hootsuite, Jul 19,
   2021, https://blog.hootsuite.com/instagram-
   hashtags/
2. Instagram (@creators), "Tips for Using Hashtags,"
   Instagram, Sep 27, 2021, https://www.instagram.
   com/p/CUV20kxvLgS/

3. #switalskimethod https://www.tiktok.
com/tag/switalskimethod

CHAPTER 10: PUBLISH

1. Anita Tai, "'The Social Dilemma' Scientist Explains
Why Social Media Is So Addictive on 'Ellen'," ET
Canada, Sep 28, 2020, https://etcanada.com/news/
696275/the-social-dilemma-scientist-explains-why-
social-media-is-so-addictive-on-ellen/

2. University of Wollongong Australia,
"Understanding your digital shadow," UOW, Apr
30, 2019, https://www.uow.edu.au/student/learning-
co-op/technology-and-software/understanding-
your-digital-shadow/

CHAPTER 11: MXLTIPLY

1. Instagram (@creators), "Tips for Getting Discovered
in the Reels Tab," Instagram, Feb 9, 2021, https://
www.instagram.com/p/CLFMSunBRXi/

2. SnapTik https://snaptik.app/

3. YouTube, "Introducing the shorter side of
YouTube," Youtube Creators, https://www.youtube.
com/creators/shorts/

4. Instagram, "Introducing Instagram Reels,"
Instagram Blog, Aug 5, 2020, https://about.
instagram.com/blog/announcements/introducing-
instagram-reels-announcement

5. Sarah Perez, "Facebook tests a new option for cross-
posting your Facebook feed posts to Instagram,"
TechCrunch, Oct 18, 2021 https://techcrunch.com/

2021/10/18/facebook-tests-cross-posting-your-facebook-feed-posts-to-instagram/

6. Facebook, "Unlock your creativity with Reels on Facebook," Meta for Creators, Sep 28, 2021, https://www.facebook.com/creators/reels-for-facebook

7. Jessica Foster, "12 Pinterest SEO Tips for High-Traffic Success," Search Engine Journal, Nov 11, 2020, https://www.searchenginejournal.com/pinterest-seo-tips/200282/

8. Pinterest, "Pinterest introduces Idea Pins globally and launches new creator discovery features," Pinterest Newsroom, May 18, 2021, https://newsroom.pinterest.com/en/post/pinterest-introduces-idea-pins-globally-and-launches-new-creator-discovery-features

9. Andrew Hutchinson, "Pinterest Launches 'Idea Pins,' a Revamped Variation on Stories," Social Media Today, May 18, 2021, https://www.socialmediatoday.com/news/pinterest-launches-idea-pins-its-revamped-variation-on-stories/

10. Katie Sehl, "Everything You Need to Know About LinkedIn Video," Hootsuite, Apr 8, 2021, https://blog.hootsuite.com/linkedin-video/

CHAPTER 12: THE SECRETS TO SOCIAL SELLING

1. Greg Jarboe, "64 Percent of Consumers Purchase After Watching Branded Social Video Content," Tubular Insights, Jun 21, 2017, https://tubularinsights.com/64-percent-viewers-purchase-social-video/

2. Jason Aten, "Steve Jobs Stole His Best Idea Ever

From Nike's Brilliant 2-Word Marketing Strategy," Inc., Oct 2, 2021, https://www.inc.com/jason-aten/ steve-jobs-stole-his-best-idea-ever-from-nikes-brilliant-2-word-marketing-strategy.html

3. Joshua VanDeBrake, "Steve Jobs' Blueprint for Revolutionary Marketing," BetterMarketing, Aug 24, 2019, https://bettermarketing.pub/steve-jobs-blueprint-for-revolutionary-marketing-b88ec38f335

4. Ann Schmidt, "Why Costco's rotisserie chicken has cost the same for 11 years," FoxBusiness, Jun 9, 2020, https://www.foxbusiness.com/money/costco-rotisserie-chicken-price

5. Russell Brunson (@russellbrunson) "a confused mind will always say, No.," Twitter, Sep 5, 2018, https://mobile.twitter.com/russellbrunson/ status/1037324548880969728

6. Daniel Keyes, "Shoppers want to find what they need in just three clicks, per a Salesforce report," Business Insider, Jun 13, 2019, https://www. businessinsider.com/shoppers-want-to-shop-in-just-three-clicks-2019-6

7. "2021 Facebook Outage," Wikipedia, updated Jan 22, 2022, https://en.wikipedia.org/ wiki/2021_Facebook_outage

8. Pamela Vaughan, "30 Thought-Provoking Lead Nurturing Stats You Can't Ignore," Hubspot, Jan 18, 2012, https://blog.hubspot.com/blog/tabid/6307/bid/ 30901/30-Thought-Provoking-Lead-Nurturing-Stats-You-Can-t-Ignore.aspx

9. Ray Edwards, "How to Write Copy That Sells: The Step-By-Step System for More Sales, to More Customers, More Often," How to Write Copy That Sells

ABOUT THE AUTHOR

Bryan Switalski is a Digital Marketing Consultant, Copywriter, Author, and Speaker. He has a passion to help purpose-driven business leaders develop effective marketing so they can step into their dreams.

His clients include best-selling author Ray Edwards (author of How to Write Copy That Sells), Creighton Arita (CEO of the 'ike Family of Companies), Meli James (co-founder of ManaUp and president of Hawaii Venture Capital Association), and many more.

Bryan is the founder of Leverage Clarity, which offers: Copywriting, Consulting and Coaching, Sales Funnel Development, Training and Instruction.

This book comes with a free Content Planner, Social Media Prompts, and other bonuses. Scan the QR code below to access your bonuses:

Printed in Great Britain
by Amazon